Pickering's
SALUTE TO THE SENTIMENTAL BLOKE

Pickering's
SALUTE TO THE SENTIMENTAL BLOKE

VERSE BY C. J. DENNIS
ILLUSTRATIONS BY PICKERING

ANGUS AND ROBERTSON PUBLISHERS

ANGUS & ROBERTSON PUBLISHERS
London • Sydney • Melbourne • Singapore • Manila

First published by Angus & Robertson Publishers, Australia, 1978

Reprinted 1979

© Illustrations, Larry Pickering 1978
© Text, Angus & Robertson Publishers 1978

National Library of Australia
Cataloguing-in-publication data

Dennis, Clarence James, 1876-1938
Pickering's Salute to The Sentimental Bloke.

ISBN 0 207 13738 2

I. Pickering, Lawrence David, 1942-, illus.
II. Title.

A821'.2

Printed in Hong Kong

CONTENTS

A SPRING SONG

The world 'as got me snouted jist a treat;
Crool Forchin's dirty left 'as smote me soul;
An' all them joys o' life I 'eld so sweet
    Is up the pole.
Fer, as the poit sez, me 'eart 'as got
The pip wiv yearnin' fer — I dunno wot.

I'm crook; me name is Mud; I've done me dash;
Me flamin' spirit's got the flamin' 'ump!
I'm longin' to let loose on somethin' rash. . . .
    Aw, I'm a chump!
I know it; but this blimed ole Springtime craze
Fair outs me, on these dilly, silly days.

The young green leaves is shootin' on the trees,
The air is like a long, cool swig o' beer,
The bonzer smell o' flow'rs is on the breeze,
    An' 'ere's me, 'ere,
Jist moochin' round like some pore, barmy coot,
Of 'ope, an' joy, an' forchin destichoot.

I've lorst me former joy in gittin' shick,
Or 'eadin' browns; I 'aven't got the 'eart
To word a tom; an', square an' all, I'm sick
    Of that cheap tart
'Oo chucks 'er carkis at a feller's 'ead
An' mauls 'im . . . Ar! I wisht that I wus dead!

*What **is** the matter wiv me? . . . I dunno.*
I got a sorter yearnin' 'ere inside,
A dead-crook sorter thing that won't let go
Or be denied—
A feelin' like I want to do a break,
An' stoush creation for some woman's sake.

The little birds is chirpin' in the nest,
The parks an' gardings is a bosker sight,
Where smilin' tarts walks up an' down, all dressed
In clobber white.
An', as their snowy forms goes steppin' by,
It seems I'm seekin' somethin' on the sly:

Somethin' or someone—I don't rightly know;
But, seems to me, I'm kind er lookin' for
A tart I knoo a 'undred years ago,
Or, maybe, more.
Wot's this I've 'eard them call that thing? . . . Geewhizz
Me ideel bit o' skirt! That's wot it is!

Me ideel tart! . . . An', bli'me, look at me!
Jist take a squiz at this, an' tell me can
Some square an' honist tom take this to be
'Er own true man?
Aw, Gawd! I'd be as true to 'er, I would—
As straight an' stiddy as . . . Ar, wot's the good?

Me, that 'as done me stretch fer stoushin' Johns,
An' spen's me leisure gittin' on the shick,
An' 'arf me nights down there, in Little Lons.,
　　Wiv Ginger Mick,
Jist 'eadin' 'em, an' doin' in me gilt.
Tough luck! I s'pose it's 'ow a man is built.

It's 'ow Gawd builds a bloke; but don't it 'urt
When 'e gits yearnin's fer this 'igher life,
On these Spring mornin's, watchin' some sweet skirt —
　　Some fucher wife —
Go sailin' by, an' turnin' on his phiz
The glarssy eye — fer bein' wot 'e is.

I've watched 'em walkin' in the gardings 'ere —
Cliners from orfices an' shops an' such;
The sorter skirts I dursn't come too near,
　　Or dare to touch.
An' when I see the kind er looks they carst. . . .
Gorstrooth! Wot is the **use** 'o me, I arst?

The little winds is stirrin' in the trees,
Where little birds is chantin' lovers' lays;
The music of the sorft an' barmy breeze . . .
　　Aw, spare me days!
If this 'ere dilly feelin' doesn't stop
I'll lose me block an' stoush some flamin' cop!

A POST~CUP TALE

I 'ad the money in me 'and!
Fair dinkum! Right there, by the stand.
I tole me wife at breakfus' time,
Straight out: "Trivalve," I sez, "is prime."
"Trivalve," I sez, an' all the week
I swear there's no one 'eard me speak
Another 'orse's name. Why, look,
I 'ad the oil straight from a Book
On Sund'y at me cousin's place
When we was torkin' of the race.
"Trivalve," 'e sez, " 'is chance is grand."
I 'ad the money in me 'and!

Fair in me 'and I 'ad the dough!
An' then a man 'as got to go —
Wot? Tough? Look, if I 'adn't met
Jim Smith (I ain't forgave 'im yet).
'E takes an' grabs me be the coat.
"Trivalve!" 'e sez. "That 'airy goat!"
(I 'ad the money in me 'and
Just makin' for the bookie's stand)
"Trivalve!" 'e sez. "Ar, turn it up!
'Ow could 'e win a flamin' cup?"
Uv course, I thought 'e muster knoo —
'Im livin' near a trainer, too.

Right 'ere, like that, fair in me fist
I 'ad the notes! An' then I missed —
Missed like a mug fair on the knock
Becos 'is maggin' done me block.

"That 'airy goat?" 'e sez. " 'E's crook!"
Fair knocked me back, 'e did, an', look,
I 'ad the money in me 'and!
Fair in me paw, an', un'erstand,
Sixes at least I coulder got —
Thirty to five, an' made a pot.
Today, I mighter been reel rich —
Rollin' in dough! Instid o' which,
'Ere's me — aw! Don't it beat the band?
I 'ad the money in me 'and!
Put me clean off. That's wot 'e did . . .
Say, could yeh len' us 'arf a quid?

CHE SWAGMAN

Oh, he was old and he was spare;
His bushy whiskers and his hair
Were all fussed up and very grey
He said he'd come a long, long way
And had a long, long way to go.
Each boot was broken at the toe,
And he'd a swag upon his back.
His billy-can, as black as black,
Was just the thing for making tea
At picnics, so it seemed to me.

'Twas hard to earn a bite of bread,
He told me. Then he shook his head,
And all the little corks that hung
Around his hat-brim danced and swung
And bobbed about his face; and when
I laughed he made them dance again.
He said they were for keeping flies —
"The pesky varmints" — from his eyes.
He called me "Codger". . . "Now you see
The best days of your life," said he.
"But days will come to bend your back,
And, when they come, keep off the track.
Keep off, young codger, if you can."
He seemed a funny sort of man.

He told me that he wanted work,
But jobs were scarce this side of Bourke,
And he supposed he'd have to go
Another fifty mile or so.
"Nigh all my life the track I've walked,"
He said. I liked the way he talked.
And oh, the places he had seen!
I don't know where he had not been—
On every road, in every town,
All through the country, up and down.
"Young codger, shun the track," he said.
And put his hand upon my head.
I noticed, then, that his old eyes
Were very blue and very wise.
"Ay, once I was a little lad,"
He said, and seemed to grow quite sad.

I sometimes think: When I'm a man,
I'll get a good black billy-can
And hang some corks around my hat,
And lead a jolly life like that.

THE INTRO

'Er name's Doreen . . . Well, spare me bloomin' days!
You could 'a' knocked me down wiv 'arf a brick!
Yes, me, that kids meself I know their ways,
An' 'as a name for smoogin' in our click!
I jist lines up an' tips the saucy wink.
But strike! The way she piled on dawg! Yer'd think
A bloke was givin' back-chat to the Queen. . . .
'Er name's Doreen.

I seen 'er in the markit first uv all,
Inspectin' brums at Steeny Isaacs' stall.
I backs me barrer in—the same ole way—
An' sez, "Wot O! It's been a bonzer day.
'Ow is it fer a walk?" . . . Oh, 'oly wars!
The sorter **look** she gimme! Jest becors
I tried to chat 'er, like you'd make a start
Wiv **any** tart.

16

An' I kin take me oaf I wus perlite,
An' never said no word that wasn't right,
An' never tried to maul 'er, or to do
A thing yeh might call crook. Ter tell yeh true,
I didn't seem to 'ave the nerve — wiv 'er.
I felt as if I couldn't go that fur,
An' start to sling off chiack like I used.
Not intrajuiced!

Nex' time I sighted 'er in Little Bourke,
Where she was in a job. I found 'er lurk
Wus pastin' labels in a pickle joint,
A game that — any'ow, that ain't the point.
Once more I tried ter chat 'er in the street,
But, bli'me! Did she turn me down a treat!
The way she tossed 'er 'ead an' swished 'er skirt!
Oh, it wus dirt!

A squarer tom, I swear, I never seen,
In all me natchril, than this 'ere Doreen.
It wer'n't no guyver neither; fer I knoo
That any other bloke 'ad Buckley's 'oo
Tried fer to pick 'er up. Yes, she wus square.
She jist sailed by an' lef me standin' there
Like any mug. Thinks I, "I'm out 'o luck,"
An' done a duck.

Well, I dunno. It's that way wiv a bloke.
If she'd ha' breasted up ter me an' spoke,
I'd thort 'er jist a commin bit er fluff,
An' then fergot about 'er, like enough.
It's jist like this. The tarts that's 'ard ter get
Makes you all 'ot to chase 'em, an' to let
The cove called Cupid get an 'ammer-lock,
An' lose yer block.

I know a bloke 'oo knows a bloke 'oo toils
In that same pickle found-ery. ('E boils
The cabbitch storks or somethink.) Anyway,
I gives me pal the orfis fer to say
'E 'as a sister in the trade 'oo's been
Out uv a job, an' wants ter meet Doreen;
Then we kin get an intro, if we've luck.
'E sez, "Ribuck."

O' course we worked the oricle; you bet!
But, struth, I ain't recovered frum it yet!
'Twas on a Saturdee, in Colluns Street,
An'—quite be accident, o' course—we meet.
Me pal 'e trots 'er up an' does the toff—
'E allus wus a bloke fer showin' off.
"This 'ere's Doreen," 'e sez. "This 'ere's the Kid."
I dips me lid.

"This 'ere's Doreen," 'e sez. I sez "Good day."
An', bli'me, I 'ad nothin' more ter say!
I couldn't speak a word, or meet 'er eye.
Clean done me block! I never been so shy
Not since I wus a tiny little cub,
An' run the rabbit to the corner pub—
Wot time the Summer days wus dry an' 'ot—
Fer my ole pot.

I dunno 'ow I done it in the end.
I reckerlect I arst ter be 'er friend;
An' tried ter play at 'andies in the park,
A thing she wouldn't sight. Aw, it's a nark!
I gotter swear when I think wot a mug
I must 'a' seemed to 'er. But still I 'ug
That promise that she give me fer the beach.
The bonzer peach!

Now, as the poit sez, the days drag by
On ledding feet. I wish't they'd do a guy.
I dunno 'ow I 'ad the nerve ter speak
An' make that meet wiv 'er fer Sundee week!
But, strike! It's funny wot a bloke'll do
When 'e's all out . . . She's gorn, when I come-to.
I'm yappin' to me cobber uv me mash. . . .
I've done me dash!

'Er name's Doreen. . . . An' me—that thort I knoo
The ways uv tarts, an' all that smoogin' game!
An' so I ort; fer ain't I known a few?
Yet some'ow . . . I dunno. It ain't the same.
*I carn't tell **wot** it is; but, all I know,*
I've dropped me bundle—an' I'm glad it's so.
Fer when I come ter think uv wot I been. . . .
'Er name's Doreen.

A MORNING SONG

The thrush is in the wattle tree, an', "O, you pretty dear!"
He's callin' to his little wife for all the bush to hear.
He's wantin' all the bush to know about his charmin' hen;
He sings it over fifty times, an' then begins again.
For it's Mornin'! Mornin'! The world is wet with dew,
With tiny drops a-twinkle where the sun comes shinin' thro'.

The thrush is in the wattle tree, red robin's underneath,
The little blue-cap's dodgin' in an' out amongst the heath;
An' they're singin', boy, they're singin' like they'd bust 'emselves to bits;
While, up above, old Laughin' Jack is havin' forty fits.
For it's Mornin'! Mornin'! The leaves are all ashine:
There's treasure all about the place; an' all of it is mine.

Oh, it's good to be a wealthy man, it's grand to be a king
With mornin' on the forest-land an' joy in everything.
It's fine to be a healthy man with healthy work to do
In the singin' land, the clean land, washed again with dew.
When sunlight slants across the trees, an' birds begin to sing,
Then kings may snore in palaces, but I'm awake—and king.

But the king must cook his breakfast, an' the king must sweep the floor;
Then out with axe on shoulder to his kingdom at the door,
His old dog sportin' on ahead, his troubles all behind,
An' joy mixed in the blood of him because the world is kind.
For it's Mornin'! Mornin'! Time to out an' strive!
Oh, there's not a thing I'm askin' else but just to be alive!

My friends are in the underbrush, my friends are in the trees,
An' merrily they welcome me with mornin' melodies.
Above, below, from bush an' bough each calls his tuneful part;
An' best of all, one trusty friend is callin' in my heart.
For it's Mornin'! Mornin'! When night's black troubles end.
An' never man was friendless yet who stayed his own good friend.

Grey thrush is in the wattle, an' it's, "O, you pretty dear!"
He's callin' to his little wife, an' don't care who should hear
In the great bush, the fresh bush, washed again with dew;
An' my axe is on my shoulder, an' there's work ahead to do.
Oh, it's Mornin'! Singing Mornin'! in the land I count the best,
An' with the heart an' mind of me I'm singin' with the rest.

⊄OOLANGI

To linger in Toolangi when the winds o' Winter blow
Is to get an aftertaste of what old Noah used to know;
And to loiter in Toolangi when the suns o' Summer bake
Is to suffer from a plethora of bullock-whip and snake;
But your heart is full of gladness and it makes your spirit sing
Just to linger in Toolangi, in Toolangi in the Spring.

Then the whip-birds wake the gullies where the wattles tell their gold
And thrilling thrushes sing again, as poets sang of old,
Of the glory of the bushland and the glamour of the scrub —
While the early-rising robin scoffs the festive homing grub
Loud laugh the Jacks, while wombats strive to sing in divers keys
(Even wombats want to warble, when the bloom is on the trees).
Then if ye'd known the joy o' life that Austral poets sing,
O' come ye to Toolangi to Toolangi in the Spring.

DOREEN

"I wish't yeh meant it, Bill." Oh, 'ow me 'eart
Went out to 'er that ev'nin' on the beach.
I knoo she weren't no ordinary tart,
My little peach!
I tell yeh, square an' all, me 'eart stood still
To 'ear 'er say, "I wish't yeh meant it, Bill."

To 'ear 'er voice! Its gentle sort o' tone,
Like soft dream-music of some Dago band.
An' me all out; an' 'oldin' in me own
'Er little 'and,
An' 'ow she blushed! O, strike! it was divine
The way she raised 'er shinin' eyes to mine.

'Er eyes! Soft in the moon; such **boshter** eyes!
An' when they sight a bloke . . . O, spare me days!
'E goes all loose inside; such glamour lies
In 'er sweet gaze.
It makes 'im all ashamed uv wot 'e's been
To look into the eyes of my Doreen.

The wet sands glistened, an' the gleamin' moon
Shone yeller on the sea, all streakin' down.
A band was playin' some soft, dreamy toon;
    An' up the town
We 'eard the distant tram-cars whir an' clash.
An' there I told 'er 'ow I'd done me dash.

"I wish't yeh meant it." 'Struth! And did I, fair?
A bloke 'ud be a dawg to kid a skirt
Like 'er. An' me well knowin' she was square.
    It 'ud be dirt!
'Ed be no man to point wiv her, an' kid.
I meant it honest; an' she knoo I did.

She knoo. I've done me block in on 'er, straight.
A cove 'as got to think some time in life
An' git some decent tart, ere it's too late,
    To be 'is wife.
But, Gawd! 'Oo would a' thort it could 'a' been
My luck to strike the likes uv 'er? . . . Doreen!

Aw, I can stand their chuckin' off, I can.
It's 'ard; an' I'd delight to take 'em on.
The dawgs! But it gets that way wiv a man
    When 'e's fair gone.
She'll sight no stoush; an' so I 'ave to take
Their mag, an' do a duck fer 'er sweet sake.

Fer 'er sweet sake I've gone and chucked it clean:
The pubs an' schools an' all that leery game.
Fer when a bloke 'as come to know Doreen,
    It ain't the same.
There's 'igher things, she sez, fer blokes to do.
An' I am 'arf believin' that it's true.

Yes, 'igher things — that wus the way she spoke;
An' when she looked at me I sort o' felt
That bosker feelin' that comes o'er a bloke,
    An' makes 'im melt;
Makes 'im all 'ot to maul 'er, an' to shove
'Is arms about 'er . . . Bl'ime? but it's love!

That's wot it is. An' when a man 'as grown
Like that 'e gets a sort o' yearn inside
To be a little 'ero on 'is own;
    An' see the pride
Glow in the eyes of 'er 'e calls 'is queen;
An' 'ear 'er say 'e is a shine champeen.

"I wish't yeh meant it," I can 'ear 'er yet,
My bit o' fluff! The moon wus shinin' bright,
Turnin' the waves all yeller where it set —
    A bonzer night!
The sparklin' sea all sort o' gold an' green;
An' on the pier the band — O, 'Ell! . . . Doreen!

THE CIRCUS

Hey, there! Hoop-la! the circus is in town!
Have you seen the elephant? Have you seen the clown?
Have you seen the dappled horse gallop round the ring?
Have you seen the acrobats on the dizzy swing?
Have you seen the tumbling men tumble up and down?
Hoop-la! Hoop-la! the circus is in town!

Hey, there! Hoop-la! Here's the circus troupe!
Here's the educated dog jumping through the hoop.
See the lady Blondin with the parasol and fan,
The lad upon the ladder and the india-rubber man.
See the joyful juggler and the boy who loops the loop.
Hey! Hey! Hey! Hey! Here's the circus troupe!

THE TRIANTIWONTIGONGOLOPE

There's a very funny insect that you do not often spy,
And it isn't quite a spider, and it isn't quite a fly;
It is something like a beetle, and a little like a bee,
But nothing like a woolly grub that climbs upon a tree.
Its name is quite a hard one, but you'll learn it soon, I hope.
So, try:
Tri-
Tri-anti-wonti-
Triantiwontigongolope.

It lives on weeds and wattle-gum, and has a funny face;
Its appetite is hearty, and its manners a disgrace.
When first you come upon it, it will give you quite a scare,
But when you look for it again you find it isn't there.
And unless you call it softly it will stay away and mope.
So, try:
Tri-
Tri-anti-wonti-
Triantiwontigongolope.

It trembles if you tickle it or tread upon its toes;
It is not an early riser, but it has a snubbish nose
If you sneer at it, or scold it, it will scuttle off in shame,
But it purrs and purrs quite proudly if you call it by its name,
And offer it some sandwiches of sealing-wax and soap.
So, try:
Tri-
Tri-anti-wonti-
Triantiwontigongolope.

But of course you haven't seen it; and I truthfully confess
That I haven't seen it either, and I don't know its address.
For there isn't such an insect, though there really might have been
If the trees and grass were purple, and the sky was bottle-green.
It's just a little joke of mine, which you'll forgive, I hope.
Oh, try!
Try!
Tri-anti-wonti-
Triantiwontigongolope.

MAR

'Er pore dear Par," she sez, " 'e kept a store";
An' then she weeps an' stares 'ard at the floor.
" 'Twas thro' 'is death," she sez, "we wus rejuiced
To this," she sez . . . An' then she weeps some more.

" 'Er Par," she sez, "me poor late 'usband, kept
An 'ay an' corn store. 'E'd no faults ixcept
'Im fallin' 'eavy orf a load o' charf
W'ich — killed 'im — on the — " 'Struth! But 'ow she wept.

She blows 'er nose an' sniffs. " 'E would 'a' made"
She sez "a lot of money in the trade.
But, 'im took orf so sudden-like, we found
'E 'adn't kept 'is life insurince paid.

"To think," she sez, "a child o' mine should be
Rejuiced to workin' in a factory!
If 'er pore Par 'e 'adn't died," she sobs . . .
I sez, "It wus a bit o' luck for me."

Then I gits red as 'ell, "That is — I mean,"
I sez, "I mighter never met Doreen
If 'e 'ad not" — an' 'ere I lose me block —
"I 'ope," I sez, " 'e snuffed it quick and clean."

An' that wus 'ow I made me first deboo.
I'd dodged it cunnin' fer a month or two.
Doreen she sez, "You'll 'ave to meet my Mar,
Some day," she sez. An' so I seen it thro'.

I'd pictered some stern female in a cap
Wot puts the fear o' Gawd into a chap.
An' 'ere she wus, aweepin' in 'er tea
An' drippin' moistcher like a leaky tap.

Two dilly sorter dawgs made outer delf
Stares 'ard at me frum orf the mantelshelf.
I seemed to symperthise wiv them there pups;
I felt so stiff an' brittle-like meself.

Clobber? Me trosso, 'ead to foot, wus noo —
Got up regardless, fer this interview.
Stiff shirt, a Yankee soot split up the back,
A tie wiv yeller spots an' stripes o' blue.

Me cuffs kep' playin' wiv me nervis fears
Me patent leathers nearly brought the tears
An' there I sits wiv, "Yes, mum. Thanks. Indeed?"
Me stand-up collar sorin' orf me ears.

"Life's 'ard," she sez, an' then she brightens up.
"Still, we 'ave alwus 'ad our bite and sup.
Doreen's been **sich** a help; she 'as indeed.
Some more tea, Willy? **'Ave** another cup."

Willy! O 'ell! 'Ere wus a flamin' pill!
A moniker that alwus makes me ill.
"If it's the same to you, mum," I replies
"I answer quicker to the name of Bill."

Up goes 'er 'ands an' eyes, "That vulgar name!"
No, Willy, but it isn't all the same,
My fucher son must be respectable."
"Orright," I sez, "I s'pose it's in the game."

"Me fucher son," she sez, "right on frum this
Must not take anythink I say amiss.
I know me jooty be me son-in-lor;
So, Willy, come an' give yer Mar a kiss."

I done it. Tho' I dunno 'ow I did.
"Dear boy," she sez, "to do as you are bid.
Be kind to 'er," she sobs, "my little girl!"
An' then I kiss Doreen. Sez she "Ah Kid!"

Doreen! Ar 'ow 'er pretty eyes did shine.
No sight on earth or 'Eaving's 'arf so fine,
An' as they looked at me she seemed to say
"I'm proud of 'im, I am, an' 'e is mine."

There wus a sorter glimmer in 'er eye,
An 'appy, nervis look, 'arf proud, 'arf shy;
I seen 'er in me mind be'ind the cups
In our own little kipsie, bye an' bye.

An' then when Mar-in-lor an' me began
To tork of 'ouse'old things an' scheme an' plan,
A sudden thort fair jolts me where I live :
"These is my wimmin folk! An' I'm a man!"

It's wot they calls responsibility.
All of a 'eap that feelin' come to me ;
An' somew'ere in me 'ead I seemed to feel
A sneakin' sort o' wish that I was free.

'Ere's me 'oo never took no 'eed o' life,
Investin' in a mar-in-lor an' wife :
Someone to battle fer besides meself,
Somethink to love an' shield frum care and strife.

It makes yeh solim when yeh come to think
Wot love and marridge means. Ar, strike me pink!
It ain't all sighs and kisses. It's yer life.
An' 'ere's me tremblin' on the bloomin' brink.

" 'Er pore dead Par," she sez, an' gulps a sob.
An' then I tells 'er 'ow I got a job,
As storeman down at Jones' printin' joint,
A decent sorter cop at fifty bob.

Then things get 'ome-like; an' we torks till late,
An' tries to tease Doreen to fix the date,
An' she gits suddin soft and tender-like,
An' cries a bit, when we parts at the gate.

An' as I'm moochin' 'omeward frum the car
A suddin notion stops me wiv a jar —
Wot if Doreen, I thinks, should grow to be,
A fat ole weepin' willer like 'er Mar!

O, 'struth! It won't bear thinkin' of! It's crook!
An' I'm a mean, unfeelin' dawg to look
At things like that. Doreen's Doreen to me,
The sweetest peach on w'ich a man wus shook.

'Er "pore dear Par" . . . I s'pose 'e 'ad 'is day,
An' kissed an' smooged an' loved 'er in 'is way.
An' wed an' took 'is chances like a man —
But, Gawd, this splicin' racket ain't all play.

Love is a gamble, an' there ain't no certs.
Some day, I s'pose, I'll git wise to the skirts,
An' learn to take the bitter wiv the sweet . . .
But, strike me purple! "Willy!" **That's** wot 'urts.

JOI, THE GLUG

The Glugs abide in a far, far land
That is partly pebbles and stones and sand,
But mainly earth of a chocolate hue,
When it isn't purple or slightly blue.
And the Glugs live there with their aunts and wives,
In draught-proof tenements all their lives.
And they climb the trees when the weather is wet,
To see how high they can really get.
Pray, don't forget,
This is chiefly done when the weather is wet.

And every shadow that flits and hides,
And every stream that glistens and glides
And laughs its way from a highland height,
All know the Glugs quite well by sight.
And they say, "Our test is the best by far;
For a Glug is a Glug; so there you are!
And they climb the trees when it drizzles or hails
To get electricity into their nails;
And the Glug that fails
Is a luckless Glug, if it drizzles or hails."

Now, the Glugs abide in the land of Gosh;
And they work all day for the sake of Splosh.
For Splosh, the First, is the nation's pride,
And King of the Glugs, on his uncle's side.
And they sleep at night, for the sake of rest;
For their doctors say this suits them best.
And they climb the trees, as a general rule,
For exercise, when the weather is cool.
They're taught at school
To climb the trees when the weather is cool.

And the whispering grass on the gay green hills,
And every cricket that skirls and shrills,
And every moonbeam, gleaming white,
All know the Glugs quite well by sight.
And they say, "It is safe, is the test we bring;
For a Glug is an awfully Gluglike thing.
And they climb the trees when there's sign of a fog,
To scan the land for a feasible dog.
They love to jog
Thro' dells in quest of a feasible dog."

The Glugs eat meals three times a day
Because their fathers ate that way.
Their grandpas said the scheme was good
To help the Glugs digest their food.
And 'tis wholesome food the Glugs have got,
For it says so plain on the tin and pot.
And they climb the trees when the weather is dry
To get a glimpse of the pale green sky.
We don't know why,
But they like to gaze on a pale green sky.

And every cloud that sails aloft,
And every breeze that blows so soft,
And every star that shines at night,
All know the Glugs quite well by sight.
For they say, "Our test, it is safe and true;
What one Glug does, the other Glugs do;
And they climb the trees when the weather is hot,
For a bird's-eye view of the garden plot.
   Of course, it's rot,
But they love that view of the garden plot."

At half-past two on a Wednesday morn
A most peculiar Glug was born;
And, later on, when he grew a man,
He scoffed and sneered at the Chosen Plan.
"It's wrong!" said this Glug, whose name was Joi.
"Bah!" said the Glugs. "He's a crazy boy!"
And they climbed the trees, as the West wind stirred,
To hark to the note of the Guffer Bird.
   It seems absurd,
But they're foolishly fond of the Guffer Bird.

And every reed that rustles and sways
By the gurgling river that plashes and plays,
And the beasts of the dread, neurotic night
All know the Glugs quite well by sight.
And, "Why," say they; "It is easily done;
For a dexter Glug's like a sinister one!"
And they climb the trees. Oh, they climb the trees!
And they bark their knuckles, and chafe their knees;
And 'tis one of the world's great mysteries
   That things like these
Get into the serious histories.

THE SPOILERS

Ye are the Great White People, masters and lords of the earth,
Spreading your stern dominion over the world's wide girth.
Here, where my fathers hunted since Time's primordial morn,
To our land's sweet, fecund places, you came with your kine and corn.
Mouthing your creed of Culture to cover a baser creed,
Your talk was of White Man's magic; but your secret god was Greed.
And now that your generations to the second, the third have run,
White Man, what of my country? Answer, what have you done?

Now the God of my Simple People was a simple, kindly God,
Meting his treasure wisely that sprang from this generous sod,
With never a beast too many and never a beast too few,
Thro' the lean years and the fruitful, he held the balance true.
Then the White Lords came in their glory; and their cry was: "More! Yet more!"
And to make them rich for a season they filched Earth's age-old store,
And they hunted my Simple People — hunters of yester-year —
And they drove us into the desert — while they wrought fresh deserts here.

They ravaged the verdant uplands and spoiled wealth ages old,
Laid waste with their pumps and sluices for a gunny-bag of gold;
They raided the primal forests and the kind, rain-bringing trees
That poured wealth over the lowlands thro' countless centuries;
They fed their kine on the grasslands, crowding them over the land,
Till blade and root in the lean years gave place to hungry sand.
Then, warned too late of their folly, the White Lords grew afraid,
And they cried to their great god Science; but Science could not aid.

This have you done to our country, lords of the air and the seas,
This to the hoarded riches of countless centuries—
Life-yielding loam, uncovered, unsheltered in the drought,
In the floods your hand unbridled, to the age-old sea drifts out.
You have sold man's one true birthright for a White Man's holiday,
And the smothering sands drift over where once green fields turn grey—
Filched by the White Man's folly to pamper the White Lords' vice;
And leave to your sons a desert where you found a paradise.

GINGER MICK ~ AN INTRODUCTION

Jist to intrajuice me cobber, an' 'is name is Ginger Mick —
A rorty boy, a naughty boy, wiv rude ixpressions thick
In 'is casu'l conversation, an' the wicked sort o' face
That gives the sudden shudders to the lor-abidin' race.

'Is name is on the records at the Melbourne City Court,
Fer doin' things an' sayin' things no reel nice feller ort;
An' 'is name is on the records uv the Army, over there,
Fer doin' things — same sort o' things that rose the Bench's 'air.

They never rung no joy-bells when 'e made 'is first de-boo;
But 'e got free edjication, w'ich they fondly shoved 'im thro';
Then turned 'im loose in Spadger's Lane to 'ang around the street
An' 'elp the cop to re-erlize the 'ardness uv 'is beat.

Then 'e quickly dropped 'is aitches, so as not to be mistook
Fer an edjicated person, 'oo 'is cobbers reckoned crook;
But 'e 'ad a trick wiv figgers that ud make a clerk look sick;
So 'e pencilled fer a bookie; an' 'e 'awked a bit, did Mick.

A bloke can't be partic'lar 'oo must battle fer a crust;
An' some, they pinch fer preference, an' some, becos they must.
When times is 'ard, an' some swell coves is richer than they ort;
Well, it's jist a little gamble fer a rise, agin the Court.

Now, Mick wus never in it as a reel perfeshnal crook,
But sometimes cops 'as slabs uv luck, so sometimes 'e wus took,
An' 'e got a repitation, thro' 'im bein' twice interned;
But 'e didn't skite about it, 'cos 'e felt it wasn't earned.

I reckerlect one time a Beak slings Mick a slab uv guff,
Wiv "Thirty days or forty bob" (Mick couldn't raise the stuff)—
An' arsts 'im where 'is conshuns is, an' w'y 'e can't be good,
An' Mick jist grins, an' takes it out, an' never understood.

An' that is orl there wus to Mick, wiv orl 'is leery ways.
If I wus up among the 'eads, wiv right to blame or praise,
Whenever some sich bloke as 'im wus tucked away fer good
I'd chalk them words above 'is 'ead: " 'E never understood."

If I wus up among the 'eads, wiv right to judge the game,
I'd look around fer chance to praise, an' sling the flamin' blame;
Fer findin' things in blokes to praise pays divvies either way;
An' wot they're blamed fer yesterd'y brings 'earty cheers to-day.

Yes, 'earty cheers frum thortless coots 'oo feel dead sure their God
Would never 'ave no time fer crooks 'oo does a stretch in quod;
'Oo reckon 'eaven is a place where orl folk tork correck,
An' Judgment, where the "vulgar" gits it solid in the neck.

An' Ginger Mick wus vulgar. 'Struth! When things wus gettin' slow
'E took to 'awkin' rabbits, w'ich is very, very low—
'E wus the sort o' bloke to watch when 'e come in yer gate:
'E 'ad a narsty fightin' face that orl nice people 'ate.

'E 'ad that narsty fightin' face that peaceful folk call grim;
But I 'ave seen it grow reel soft when kiddies spoke to 'im.
'E 'ad them narsty sullen eyes that nice folk can't enjure;
But I 'ave seen a smile in 'em that made our frien'ship sure.

There's men 'oo never knoo ole Mick, an' passed 'im in the street,
An' looks away an' sez, "See 'im? A narsty chap to meet!
    'E'd be an ugly customer alone an' after dark!"
An' Mick, 'e'd twitch 'is jor at 'em, 'arf earnest, 'arf a lark.

That wus the sort o' character that Mick earned be 'is looks.
The talk uv 'im, the walk uv 'im, put 'im among the crooks.
An' Mick, 'e looks on swank an' style as jist a lot o' flam,
An' snouted them that snouted 'im, an' never give a dam.

But spite uv orl 'is 'ulkin' frame, an' langwidge flowin' free
I seen the thing inside uv Mick that made 'im good to me.
An' spite uv orl the sneerin' ways that leery blokes imploy,
    I knoo 'im jist fer wot 'e wus — a big, soft-'earted boy.

Fer when a bloke 'as come to be reel cobbers wiv a bloke,
They sorter swap good fellership wivout words bein' spoke.
    I never slung no guff to Mick, 'e never smooged to me,
But we could smoke, an' 'old our jor, an' be reel company.

There 'as bin times that 'e would curse to 'ave recalled by me,
When I 'ave seen 'im doin' things that coves calls charity;
An' there's been times, an' frequent times, in spite uv orl 'is looks,
When I 'ave 'eard 'im sayin' things that blokes shoves inter books.

But Ginger Mick was Ginger Mick — a leery boy, fer keeps,
'Oo 'owled "Wile Rabbee!" in the streets, in tones that give yeh creeps.
'E never planned 'is mode uv life, nor chose the Lane fer lair,
No more than 'e designed 'is chiv or colour uv 'is 'air.

So Ginger 'awked, an' Ginger pinched, an' Ginger went to quod,
An' never thort to waste 'is time in blamin' man or God —
An' then there came the Call uv Stoush, or Jooty — wot's a name?
An' Ginger cocked 'is 'ear to it, an' found 'is flamin' game.

I intrajuice me cobber 'ere; an' don't make no ixcuse
To any culchered click that it's a peb I intrajuice.
I dunno wot 'is ratin' wus in this 'ere soshul plan;
I only know, inside o' me, I intrajuice a man.

BEEF TEA

She never magged; she never said no word;
But sat an' looked at me an' never stirred.
I could 'a' bluffed it out if she 'ad been
Fair narked, an' let me 'ave it wiv 'er tongue,
But silence told me 'ow 'er 'eart wus wrung.
   Poor 'urt Doreen!
Gorstruth! I'd sooner fight wiv fifty men
Than git one look like that frum 'er agen!

She never moved; she never spoke no word;
That 'urt look in 'er eyes, like some scared bird:
" 'Ere is the man I loved," it seemed to say.
" 'E's mine, this crawlin' thing, an' I'm 'is wife;
Tied up fer good; an' orl me joy in life
   Is chucked away!"
If she 'ad bashed me I'd 'a felt no 'urt!
But 'ere she treats me like—like I wus dirt.

'Ow is a man to guard agen that look?
Fer other wimmin, when the'r blokes go crook,
An' lobs 'ome wiv the wages uv a jag,
They smashes things an' carries on a treat
An' 'owls an' scolds an' wakes the bloomin' street
   Wiv noisy mag.
But 'er—she never speaks; she never stirs . . .
I drops me bundle . . . An' the game is 'ers.

Jist two months wed! Eight weeks uv married bliss
Wiv my Doreen, an' now it's come to this!
Wot wus I thinkin' uv? Gawd! I ain't fit
To kiss the place 'er little feet 'as been!
'Er that I called me wife, me own Doreen!
   Fond dreams 'as flit;
Love's done a bunk, an' joy is up the pole;
An' shame an' sorrer's roostin' in me soul.

'Twus orl becors uv Ginger Mick—the cow!
(I wish't I 'ad 'im 'ere to deal wiv now!
I'd pass 'im one, I would! 'E ain't no man!)
I meets 'im Choosdee ev'nin' up the town.
"Wot O," 'e chips me. "Kin yeh keep one down?"
                    I sez I can.
We 'as a couple; then meets three er four
Flash coves I useter know, an' 'as some more.

    " 'Ow are yeh on a little gamble, Kid?"
Sez Ginger Mick. "Lars night I'm on four quid.
Come 'round an' try yer luck at Steeny's school."
"No," sez me conscience. Then I thinks, "Why not?
An' buy 'er presents if I wins a pot?
                    A blazin' fool
I wus. Fer 'arf a mo' I 'as a fight;
Then conscience skies the wipe . . . Sez I "Orright."

    Ten minutes later I was back once more,
Kip in me 'and, on Steeny Isaac's floor,
Me luck was in an' I wus 'eadin' good.
Yes, back agen amongst the same old crew!
An' orl the time down in me 'eart I knew
                    I never should . . .
Nex' thing I knows it's after two o'clock—
Two in the mornin'! An' I've done me block!

    "Wot odds?" I thinks. "I'm in fer it orright."
An' so I stops an' gambles orl the night;
An' bribes me conscience wiv the gilt I wins.
But when I comes out in the cold, 'ard dawn
I know I've crooled me pitch; me soul's in pawn.
                    My flamin' sins
They 'its me in a 'eap right where I live;
Fer I 'ave broke the solim vow I give.

She never magged; she never said no word.
An' when I speaks, it seems she never 'eard.
I could 'a' sung a nim, I feels so gay!
If she 'ad only roused I might 'a' smiled.
She jist seems 'urt an' crushed; not even riled.
I turns away,
An' yanks me carkis out into the yard,
Like some whipped pup; an' kicks meself reel 'ard.

An' then, I sneaks to bed, an' feels dead crook.
Fer golden quids I couldn't face that look —
That trouble in the eyes uv my Doreen.
Aw, strike! Wot made me go an' do this thing?
I feel jist like a chewed up bit of string,
An' rotten mean!
Fer 'arf an hour I lies there feelin' cheap;
An' then I s'pose, I muster fell asleep. . . .

" 'Ere, Kid, drink this". . . I wakes, an' lifts me 'ead,
An' sees 'er standin' there beside the bed;
A basin in 'er 'ands; an' in 'er eyes —
(Eyes that wiv unshed tears is shinin' wet) —
The sorter look I never shall ferget,
Until I dies.
" 'Ere, Kid, drink this," she sez, an' smiles at me.
I looks — an' spare me days! **It was beef tea!**

Beef tea! She treats me like a hinvaleed!
Me! that 'as caused 'er lovin' 'eart to bleed.
It 'urts me worse than maggin' fer a week!
'Er! 'oo 'ad right to turn dead sour on me,
Fergives like that, an' feeds me wiv beef tea . . .
I tries to speak;
An' then — I ain't ashamed o' wot I did —
I 'ides me face . . . an' blubbers like a kid.

THE VISION

Of things that roam about the bush I ain't got many fears,
For I knows their ways an' habits, an' I've chummed with them for years.
For man or beast or gully ghost I've pluck enough to spare;
But I draws the line at visions with the sunlight in their hair.

I was feelin' fine this mornin' when I started out to work;
An' I caught myself high-steppin' with a boastful sort of jerk;
With my head a trifle higher an' my eye a little stern.
I thought the world was mine for keeps; but I'd a lot to learn.

I was workin' at the rip saw; for the boss had called me in
From the peaceful bush an' quiet to the sawmill's fuss an' din;
An' there he put me tailin' out — a game I never like;
But, "Likin' isn't gettin' in the bush," says Daddy Pike.

I was workin' at the rip saw, cursin' at my achin' back,
When I saw the blessed vision comin' down the log-yard track.
There were others in the party, but the one that got my stare
Was her with two brown, laughin' eyes an' sunlight in her hair.

"More visitors!" growled old man Pike. "Another city push.
I'll bet a quid they ask us why we 'spoil the lovely bush'."
I hardly heard him saying it, for like a fool I stand,
My eyes full of the vision an' a batten in my hand.

"You gone to sleep?" the sawyer said. "What's got you mesmerized?"
I start to work like fury, but my thoughts can't be disguised.
"Oh, Jim's gone dippy with the Spring," replies old Pike an' grins.
I turn to answer dignified; but trip, an' bark my shins.

Next thing I know the boss is there, an' talkin' fine an' good,
Explainin' to the visitors how trees are made of wood.
They murmur things like "Marvellous!" an' "What a monster tree!"
An' then the one with sunlit hair comes right bang up to me.

"I saw you fall," she sort of sung: you couldn't say she talked,
For her voice had springtime in it, like the way she looked an' walked.
"I saw you fall," she sung at me. "I hope you were not hurt?"
An' suddenly I was aware I wore my oldest shirt.

"It never hurt me half as much as your two smilin' eyes."
That's how I could have answered her — an' watched old Pike's surprise —
"It never harmed me half as much as standin' here like this
With tattered shirt an' grimy hands" . . . But I just says, "No, Miss."

"Oh, no," I says. "We're pretty hard, an' have to take them cracks."
(But, just to see her sudden smile, made me as soft as wax.)
"You're strong," she smiles. I answers, "Oh, I'm pretty strong, all right."
An' close behind I heard old Pike observin', "Hear 'im skite!"

That finished me. I lost what little nerve I had, an' grew
Dead certain that I looked a fool, an' that she thought so, too.
She talked some more; but I can't tell what other things she said —
I went all cold, except my ears, an' they were burnin' red.

I only know her eyes were soft, her voice was kind an' low.
I never spoke another word exceptin' "Yes" an' "No".
I never felt a bigger chump in all my livin' days,
Well knowin' I was gettin' worse at every word she says.

An' when the knock-off whistle blew, Ben Murray he came by,
An' says he'd like a private talk; but, "Pickle it," says I.
" 'Twill have to keep till later on." He answers, "As you like."
Soon after that I saw him talkin' earnest with old Pike.

If I'd been right, I might have known there's somethin' in the air
By the way the blokes were actin'; but a fat lot did I care.
Swell visions an' the deadly pip was what was wrong with me.
I slung a word to my old dog, an' we trudged home to tea.

An' after, in the same old way, we sits beside the fire,
To have a talk, my dog an' me, on fools an' vain desire.
I tell him I'm a silly chump to think the things I do;
An', with a waggle of his tail, he says he thinks so too.

I tell him I suppose she's rich, or so she seems to be;
Most likely some reel city swell—an' he don't disagree.
I says to him the chances are I'll not see her no more.
Then he gives me a funny look, an' curls up on the floor.

But I was slow to take the tip, an' went on talkin' rot
About injustice in the world, an' boiled up good an' hot.
I spouts of wrongs of workin' men an' how our rulers fail.
His eyes are shut, but he just seconds motions with his tail.

All beauty's only for the rich, all times, an' every way.
The toilers just take what is left, as I've heard Murray say
When he's been talkin' to the boys about the workers' rights,
An' spoutin' of equality, down at the huts, of nights.

I turned the social system inside-out for my old dog,
Tho' he don't seem much entertained, but lies there like a log.
I spoke of common people's wrongs — especially of mine;
But when I came to mention love I thought I heard him whine.

But I went on, an' said straight out that, tho' I seemed above
Such nonsense once, I'd changed a bit, an' I believed in love.
I said love was a splendid thing! . . . Then, true as I am born,
He rose, an' yawned, an' shut me up with one crook glance of scorn.

It's bad enough to be a bloke without one reel close friend;
But when your dog gives you the bird it's pretty near the end.
Ashamed, I sneaked away to bunk; an' fell to dreamin' there
Of a little brown-eyed vision with the sunlight in her hair.

WAR

'E sez to me, "Wot's orl this flamin' war?
The papers torks uv nothin' else but scraps.
An' wot's ole England got snake-'eaded for?
An' wot's the strength uv callin' out our chaps?"
'E sez to me, "Struth! Don't she rule the sea?
Wot does she want wiv us?" 'e sez to me.

Ole Ginger Mick is loadin' up 'is truck
One mornin' in the markit feelin' sore.
'E sez to me, "Well, mate, I've done me luck;
An' Rose is arstin', 'Wot about this war?'
I'm gone a tenner at the two-up school;
The game is crook, an' Rose is turnin' cool."

'E sez to me, " 'Ow is it fer a beer?"
I tips 'im 'ow I've told me wife, Doreen,
That when I comes down to the markit 'ere
I dodges pubs, an' chucks the tipple, clean.
    Wiv 'er an' kid alone up on the farm
    She's full uv fancies that I'll come to 'arm.

" 'Enpecked!" 'e sez. An' then, "Ar, I dunno.
I wouldn't mind if I wus in yer place.
I've 'arf a mind to give cold tea a go —
It's no game, pourin' snake-juice in yer face.
    But, lad, I 'ave to, wiv the thirst I got:
    I'm goin' over now to stop a pot."

'E goes acrost to find a pint a 'ome;
An' meets a pal an' keeps another down.
Ten minutes later, when 'e starts to roam
Back to the markit, wiv an ugly frown,
'E sprags a soljer bloke 'oo's passin' by,
An' sez 'e'd like to dot 'im in the eye.

"Your sort," sez Mick, "don't know yer silly mind!
They lead yeh like a sheep; it's time yeh woke—
The 'eads is makin' piles out uv your kind!"
"Aw, git yer 'ead read!" sez the soljer bloke.
'Struth! 'e wus willin' wus that Kharki chap;
I 'ad me work cut out to stop a scrap.

An' as the soljer fades acrost the street,
Mick strikes a light an' sits down on 'is truck,
An' chews 'is fag—a sign 'is nerve is beat—
An' swears a bit, an' sez 'e's done 'is luck.
'E grouches there ten minutes, maybe more,
Then sez quite sudden, **Blarst the flamin' war!**

Jist then a motor car goes glidin' by
Wiv two fat toffs be'ind two fat cigars;
Mick twigs 'em frum the corner uv 'is eye—
"I 'ope," 'e sez, "the 'Uns don't git **my** cars.
Me di'mons, too, don't let me sleep a wink . . .
Ar, 'Struth! I'd fight fer that sort—**I don't** think."

Then Mick gits up an' starts another fag.
"Ar, well," 'e sez, "it's no affair uv mine,
If I don't work they'd pinch me on the vag;
But I'm not keen to fight so toffs kin dine
On pickled olives . . . **Blarst** the flamin' war!
I ain't got nothin' worth the fightin' for.

"So long," 'e sez. "I got ter trade me stock;
An' when yeh 'ear I've took a soljer's job
I give yeh leave to say I've done me block
An' got a flock uv weevils in me knob."
An' then, orf-'anded-like, 'e arsts me: "Say,
Wot are they slingin' soljers fer their pay?"

I tells 'im; an' 'e sez to me, "So long.
Some day this rabbit trade will git me beat."
An' Ginger Mick shoves thro' the markit throng,
An' gits 'is barrer out into the street.
An', as 'e goes, I 'ears 'is gentle roar:
Rabbee! Wile Rabbee! . . . Blarst the flamin' war!"

GREEN WALLS

I love all gum-trees well. But, best of all,
I love the tough old warriors that tower
About these lawns, to make a great green wall
And guard, like sentries, this exotic bower
Of shrub and fern and flower.
These are my land's own sons, lean, straight and tall,
Where crimson parrots and grey gang-gangs call
Thro' many a sunlit hour.

My friends, these grave old veterans, scarred and stern,
Changeless throughout the changing seasons they.
But at their knees their tall sons lift and yearn—
Slim spars and saplings—prone to sport and sway
Like carefree boys at play;
Waxing in beauty when their young locks turn
To crimson, and, like beacon fires burn
To deck Spring's holiday.

I think of Anzacs when the dusk comes down
Upon the gums—of Anzacs tough and tall.
Guarding this gateway, Diggers strong and brown.
And when, thro' Winter's thunderings, sounds their call,
Like Anzacs, too, they fall . . .
Their ranks grow thin upon the hill's high crown:
My sentinels! But, where those ramparts frown,
Their stout sons mend the wall.

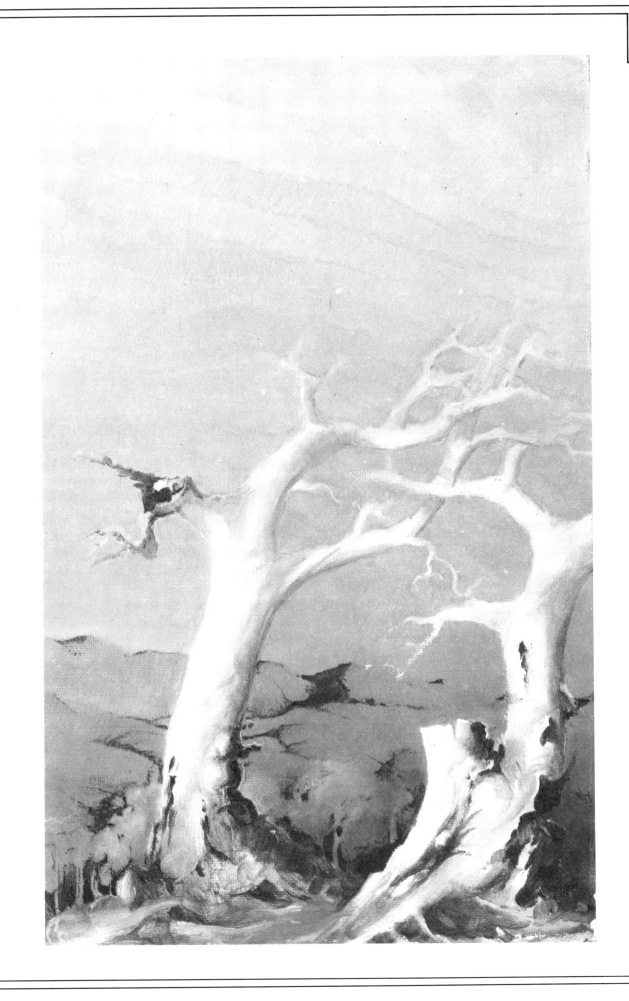

THE SILENT MEMBER

He lived in Mundaloo, and Bill McClosky was his name,
But folks that knew him well had little knowledge of that same;
For he some'ow lost his surname, and he had so much to say—
He was called "The Silent Member" in a mild, sarcastic way.

He could talk on any subject—from the weather and the crops
To astronomy and Euclid, and he never minded stops;
And the lack of a companion didn't lay him on the shelf,
For he'd stand before a looking-glass and argue with himself.

He would talk for hours on lit'rature, or calves, or art, or wheat;
There was not a bally subject you could say had got him beat;
And when strangers brought up topics that they reckoned he would baulk,
He'd remark, "I never heard of that." But all the same—he'd talk.

He'd talk at christ'nings by the yard; at weddings by the mile;
And he used to pride himself upon his choice of words and style.
In a funeral procession his remarks would never end
On the qualities and virtues of the dear departed friend.

We got quite used to hearing him, and no one seemed to care —
In fact, no happ'ning seemed complete unless his voice was there.
For close on thirty year he talked, and none could talk him down,
Until one day an agent for insurance struck the town.

Well, we knew The Silent Member, and we knew what he could do,
And it wasn't very long before we knew the agent, too,
As a crack long-distance talker that was pretty hard to catch;
So we called a hasty meeting and decided on a match.

Of course, we didn't tell them we were putting up the game;
But we fixed it up between us, and made bets upon the same.
We named a time-keep and a referee to see it through;
Then strolled around, just casual, and introduced the two.

The agent got first off the mark, while our man stood and grinned;
He talked for just one solid hour, then stopped to get his wind.
"Yes; but —" sez Bill; that's all he said; he couldn't say no more;
The agent got right in again, and fairly held the floor.

On policies, and bonuses, and premiums, and all that,
He talked and talked until we thought he had our man out flat.
"I think —" Bill got in edgeways, but that there insurance chap
Just filled himself with atmosphere, and took the second lap.

I saw our man was getting dazed, and sort of hypnotized,
And they oughter pulled the agent up right there, as I advised.
"See here—" Bill started, husky; but the agent came again,
And talked right on for four hours good—from six o'clock to ten.

Then Bill began to crumple up, and weaken at the knees,
When all at once he ups and shouts, "Here, give a bloke a breeze!
Just take a pull for half a tick and let me have the floor,
And I'll take out a policy." The agent said no more.

The Silent Member swallowed hard, then coughed and cleared his throat,
But not a single word would come—no; not a blessed note.
His face looked something dreadful—such a look of pained dismay;
Then he gave us one pathetic glance, and turned, and walked away.

He's hardly spoken since that day—not more than "Yes" or "No".
We miss his voice a good bit, too; the town seems rather slow.
He was called "The Silent Member" just sarcastic, I'll allow;
But since that agent handled him it sort o' fits him now.

WASHING DAY

The little gipsy vi'lits, they wus peepin' thro' the green
As she come walkin' in the grass, me little wife, Doreen.
The sun shone on the sassafras, where thrushes sung a bar;
The 'ope an' worry uv our lives was yellin' fer 'is Mar.
I watched 'er comin' down the green; the sun wus on 'er 'air—
Jist the woman that I marri'd, when me luck wus 'eadin' fair.

I seen 'er walkin' in the sun that lit our little farm:
She 'ad three clothes-pegs in 'er mouth, an' washin' on 'er arm—
Three clothes-pegs, fer I counted 'em, an' watched 'er as she come;
"The stove-wood's low," she mumbles, "an' young Bill 'as cut 'is thumb."
Now, it weren't no giddy love-speech, but it seemed to take me straight
Back to the time I kissed 'er first beside 'er mother's gate.

Six years uv wedded life we've 'ad, an' still me dreams is sweet . . .
Aw, them bonzer little vi'lits, they wus smilin' round me feet.
An' wot's a bit uv stove-wood count, wiv paddicks grinnin' green,
When a bloke gits on to dreamin' uv the old days an' Doreen—
The days I thort I snared a saint; but since I've understood
I 'ave wed a dinkum woman, which is fifty times as good.

I 'ave wed a dinkum woman, an' she's give me eyes to see—
Oh, I ain't been mollycoddled, an' there ain't no fluff on me!
But days when I wus down an' out she seemed so 'igh above;
An' a saint is made fer worship, but a woman's made fer love.
An' a bloke is growin' richer as sich things 'e comes to know . . .
(She pegs another sheet an' sez, "The stove-wood's gittin' low.")

A bloke 'e learns a lot uv things in six years wiv a tart;
But thrushes in the sassafras ain't singin' like me 'eart.
'Tis the thrushes 'oo 'ave tort me in their choonful sort o' way
That it's best to take things singin' as yeh meet 'em day be day;
Fer I wed a reel, live woman, wiv a woman's 'appy knack
Uv torkin' reason inside out an' logic front to back.

An' I like it. 'Struth, I like it! Fer a wax doll in a 'ome,
She'd give a man the flamin' pip an' longin's fer to roam.
Aw, I ain't no silk-sock sonkie 'oo ab'ors the rood an' rough;
Fer, city-born an' gutter-bred, me schoolin' it wus tough.
An' I like the dinkum woman 'oo . . . (She jerks the clothes-prop, so,
An' sez, so sweet an' dangerous, "The stove-wood's gittin' low.")

See, I've studied men in cities, an' I've studied 'em out 'ere;
I've seen 'em 'ard thro' piety an' seen 'em kind thro' beer.
I've seen the meanest doin' deeds to make the angels smile,
An' watched the proudest playin' games that crooks 'ud reckon vile.
I 'ave studied 'em in bunches, an' I've read 'em one be one,
An' there isn't much between 'em when the 'ole thing's said an' done.

An' I've sort o' studied wimmin—fer I've met a tidy few—
An' there's times, when I wus younger, when I kids meself I knew.
But 'im 'oo 'opes to count the stars or measure up the sea,
'E kin 'ave a shot at woman, fer she's fairly flummoxed me . . .
("I'll 'ave to 'ave **some** wood," she sez, an' sez it most perlite
An' secret to a pair uv socks; an' jams a peg in, tight.)

Now, a woman, she's a woman. I 'ave fixed that fer a cert.
They're jist as like as rows uv peas from 'at to 'em uv skirt.
An' then, they're all so different, yeh find, before yeh've done,
The more yeh know uv all uv 'em the less yeh know uv one.
An' then, the more yeh know uv one . . . (She gives 'er 'air a touch:
"The stove-wood's nearly done," she sez. "Not that it matters **much**!")

The little gipsy vi'lits, they wus smilin' round me feet.
An' this dreamin' dilly day-dreams on a Summer day wus sweet.
I 'eaves me frame frum orf the fence, an' grabs me little axe;
But, when I'm 'arf way to the shed, she stops me in me tracks.
"Yer lunch is ready. That ole wood kin easy wait a while."
Strike! I'm marri'd to a woman . . . But she never seen me smile.

THE ROAD'S END

Old Ben, the pensioner, is going down to die.
Huddled in the mail-car, he turns a wistful eye
On this familiar forest scene, the wooded mountain wall;
And nought could lure him from it save the last stern call.
He has loved it with a fierce love no reason comprehends;
The great gums, the green ways, the rough bush friends.
But doctor says his tough old heart at last has let him down;
So he's off to be "patched up a bit" in hospital in town.

"Patched up a bit" . . . He'd heard that talk when they took Badger Jack,
And Charlie Clem, and Lame Mick. But none of these came back.
Was it Mick went first? Or Charlie? (Lordy, Lord! How men forget.)
And now they're taking Ben away; and Ben not eighty yet.
The youngest, he, of six old hulks; and three have gone away;
Till now there's only George Jones left, and old Pete Parraday—
His oldest friend, Pete Parraday, who has his dog to mind.
The cruellest break of all, that was—leaving his dog behind.

Old Ben, the pensioner, sits huddled in the car;
And his filmed eyes seek the skyline where the timbered ranges are—
This kind, green place of singing birds, of tree and scrubland dense.
He hears their words of forced good cheer and jovial pretence:
Says old George Jones, "In hospital you'll get real proper care."
"An' mind," says Pete, "no sparkin' with them pretty nurses there.
Why, man, you'll be a two-year-old when you come back agen."
"You keep your eye on my ole dawg, an' feed 'im good," pipes Ben.

Then, "All aboard!" the mailman shouts "Now, Ben, mind them old bones!"
A hand-clasp from Pete Parraday, a pat from old George Jones,
And Ben, the pensioner, goes off on his last pilgrimage . . .
"Broke up reel fast," growls old George Jones, "considerin' his age.
Hey! Don't let that dawg foller him! Here, Rover, you behave."
They watch the sick man turn about, and feebly try to wave.
Swiftly the car speeds round the bend; the echoes die away . . .
"Me next? Or maybe you, George," says old Pete Parraday.

"A GALLANT GENTLEMAN"

A month ago the world grew grey fer me;
A month ago the light went out fer Rose.
To 'er they broke it gentle as might be;
But fer 'is pal 'twus one uv them swift blows
That stops the 'eart-beat; fer to me it came
Jist, "Killed in Action", an', beneath 'is name.

'Ow many times 'ave I sat dreamin' 'ere
An' seen the boys returnin', gay an' proud.
I've seen the greetin's, 'eard 'is rousin' cheer,
An' watched ole Mick come stridin' thro' the crowd.
'Ow many times 'ave I sat in this chair
An' seen 'is 'ard chiv grinnin' over there.

'E's laughed, an' told me stories uv the war.
Changed some 'e looked, but still the same ole Mick,
Keener an' cleaner than 'e wus before;
'E's took me 'and, an' said 'e's in great nick.
Sich wus the dreamin's uv a fool 'oo tried
To jist crack 'ardy, an' 'old gloom aside.

An' now—well, wot's the odds? I'm only one;
One out uv many 'oo 'as lost a friend.
Manlike, I'll bounce again, an' find me fun;
But fer poor Rose it seems the bitter end.
Fer Rose, an' sich as Rose, when one man dies
It seems the world goes black before their eyes.

A parson cove he broke the noos to Rose—
A friend uv mine, a bloke wiv snowy 'air
An' gentle, soothin' sort o' ways, 'oo goes
Thro' life jist 'umpin' others' loads uv care.
Instid uv Mick—jist one rough soljer lad—
Yeh'd think 'e'd lost the dearest friend 'e 'ad.

But 'ow kin blows be sof'n'd sich as that?
Rose took it as 'er sort must take sich things.
An' if the jolt uv it 'as knocked me flat,
Well, 'oo is there to blame 'er if it brings
Black thorts that comes to women when they frets,
An' makes 'er tork wild tork an' foolish threats?

An' then there comes the letter that wus sent
To give the strength uv Ginger's passin' out —
A long, straight letter frum a bloke called Trent;
'Tain't no use tellin' wot it's orl about:
There's things that's in it I kin see quite clear
Ole Ginger Mick ud be ashamed to 'ear.

Things praisin' 'im, that pore ole Mick ud say
Wus comin' it too 'ot; fer, spare me days!
I well remember that 'e 'ad a way
Uv curlin' up when 'e wus slung bokays.
An' Trent 'e seems to think that in some way
'E owes Mick somethin' that 'e can't repay.

Well, p'raps 'e does; an' in the note 'e sends
'E arsts if Mick 'as people 'e kin find.
Fer Trent's an English toff wiv swanky friends,
An' wants to 'elp wot Ginger's left be'ind.
'E sez strange things in this 'ere note 'e sends:
"He was a gallant gentleman," it ends.

A gallant gentleman! Well, I dunno.
I 'ardly think that Mick ud like that name.
But this 'ere Trent's a toff, an' ort to know
The breedin' uv the stock frum which 'e came.
Gallant an' game Mick might 'a' bin; but then —
Lord! Fancy 'im among the gentlemen!

The way 'e died . . . Gawd! but it makes me proud
I ever 'eld 'is 'and, to read that tale.
An' Trent is one uv that 'igh-steppin' crowd
That don't sling praise around be ev'ry mail.
To 'im it seemed some great 'eroic lurk;
But Mick, I know, jist took it wiv 'is work.

Trent tells 'ow, when they found 'im, near the end,
'E starts a fag an' grins orl bright an' gay.
An' when they arsts fer messages to send
To friends, 'is look goes dreamin' far away.
"Look after Rose," 'e sez, "when I move on.
Look after . . . Rose . . . Mafeesh!" An' 'e wus gone.

"We buried 'im," sez Trent, "down by the beach.
We put mimosa on the mound uv sand
Above 'im. 'Twus the nearest thing in reach
To golden wattle uv 'is native land.
But never wus the fairest wattle wreath
More golden than the 'eart uv 'im beneath."

A gallant gentleman . . . Well, let it go.
They sez they've put them words above 'is 'ead,
Out there where lonely graves stretch in a row;
But Mick 'e'll never mind it now 'e's dead.
An' where 'e's gone, when they weigh praise an' blame,
P'raps gentlemen an' men is much the same.

A month ago, fer me the world grew grey;
A month ago the light went out fer Rose;
Becos one common soljer crossed the way,
Leavin' a common message as 'e goes.
But ev'ry dyin' soljer's 'ope lies there:
"Look after Rose. Mafeesh!" Gawd! It's a pray'r!

That's wot it is; an' when yeh sort it out,
Shuttin' year ears to orl the sounds o' strife
The shouts, the cheers, the curses — 'oo kin doubt
The claims uv women; mother, sweet'eart, wife?
An' 'oos to 'ear our soljers' dyin' wish?
An' 'oo's to 'eed? . . . "Look after Rose . . . Mafeesh!"

TO A DEAD MATE
(HENRY LAWSON)

There's many a man who rides today
In the lonely, far out-back;
There's many a man who makes his way
On a dusty bushland track;
There's many a man in bush and town
Who mourns for a good mate gone;
There are eyes grown sad and heads cast down
Since Henry has passed on.

A mate he was, and a mate to love,
For mateship was his creed;
With a strong, true heart and a soul above
This sad world's sordid greed.
He lived as a mate, and wrote as a mate
Of the things which he believed.
Now many a good man mourns his fate,
And he leaves a nation grieved.

True champion he of the lame and halt;
True knight of the poor was he,
Who could e'er excuse a brother's fault
With a ready sympathy.
He suffered much, and much he toiled,
With his hand e'er for the right:
And he dreamed and planned while the billy boiled
In the bushland camp at night.

Joe Wilson and his mates are sad,
And the tears of bushwives fall,
For the kindly heart that Henry had
Had made him loved of all.
There's many a man who rides today,
Cast down and sore oppressed;
And thro' the land I hear them say:
"Pass, Henry, to your rest."

A DIGGER'S TALE

" 'My oath!' the Duchess sez. 'You'd not ixpect
Sich things as that. Yeh don't mean kangaroos?
Go hon!' she sez, or words to that effect
(It's 'ard to imitate the speech they use)
I tells 'er, 'Straight; I drives 'em four-in-'and
'Ome in my land.'

"You 'ear a lot," sez little Digger Smith,
"About 'ow English swells is so stand-off.
Don't yeh believe it; it's a silly myth.
I've been reel cobbers with the British toff
While I'm on leave; for Blighty liked our crowd,
An' done us proud.

"Us Aussies was the goods in London town
When I was there. If they jist twigged yer 'at
The Dooks would ask yeh could yeh keep one down,
An' Earls would 'ang out 'Welcome' on the mat,
An' sling yeh invites to their stately 'alls
For fancy balls.

"This Duchess — I ain't quite sure uv 'er rank;
She might uv been a Peeress. I dunno.
I meets 'er 'usband first. 'E owns a bank,
I 'eard, an' 'arf a dozen mints or so.
A dinkum toff. 'E sez, 'Come 'ome with me
An' 'ave some tea.'

"That's 'ow I met this Duchess Wot's-er-name—
Or Countess—never mind 'er moniker;
I ain't no 'and at this 'ere title game—
An' right away, I was reel pals with 'er.
'Now, tell me all about yer 'ome,' sez she,
An' smiles at me.

"That knocks me out. I know it ain't no good
Paintin' word-picters uv the things I done
Out 'ome 'ere, barrackin' for Collin'wood,
Or puntin' on the flat at Flemington.
I know this Baroness uv Wot-yeh-call
Wants somethin' tall.

"I thinks reel 'ard; an' then I lets it go.
. I tells 'er, out at Richmond, on me Run—
A little place uv ten square mile or so—
I'm breedin' boomerangs; which is reel fun,
When I ain't troubled by the wild Jonops
That eats me crops.

"I talks about the wondrous Boshter Bird
That builds 'er nest up in the Cobber Tree,
An' 'atches our 'er young on May the third,
Stric' to the minute, jist at 'arf pas' three.
'Er eyes get big. She sez, 'Can it be true?'
'Er eyes was blue.

"An' then I speaks uv sport, an' tells 'er 'ow
In 'untin our wild Wowsers we imploy
Large packs uv Barrackers, an' 'ow their row
Wakes echoes in the forests uv Fitzroy,
Where lurks the deadly Shicker Snake 'oo's breath
Is certain death.

"I'm goin' on to talk uv kangaroos,
An' 'ow I used to drive 'em four-in-'and.
'Wot?' sez the Marchioness. 'Them things in Zoos
That 'ops about? I've seen 'em in the Strand
In double 'arness; but I ain't seen four.
Tell me some more.'

"I baulks a bit at that; an' she sez, 'Well,
There ain't no cause at all for you to feel
Modest about the things you 'ave to tell;
An' wot yeh say sounds wonderfully reel.
Your talk'—an' 'ere I seen 'er eyelids flick—
'Makes me 'omesick.'

" 'I reckerlect,' she sez—'Now, let me see—
In Gippsland, long ago, when I was young,
I 'ad a little pet Cooroboree'
(I sits up in me chair like I was stung,)
'On its 'ind legs,' she sez, 'it used to stand.
Fed from me 'and.'

"Uv course, I threw me alley in right there.
This Princess was a dinkum Aussie girl.
I can't do nothin' else but sit an' stare,
Thinkin' so rapid that me 'air roots curl.
But 'er? She sez, 'I ain't 'eard talk so good
Since my child'ood.

" 'I wish,' sez she, 'I could be back again
Beneath the wattle an' that great blue sky.
It's like a breath uv 'ome to meet you men.
You've done reel well,' she sez. 'Don't you be shy.
When yer in Blighty once again,' sez she,
'Come an' see me.'

"I don't see 'er no more; 'cos I stopped one.
But, 'fore I sails, I gits a billy doo
Which sez, 'Give my love to the dear ole Sun,
An' take an exile's blessin' 'ome with you.
An' if you 'ave some boomerangs to spare,
Save me a pair.

" 'I'd like to see 'em play about,' she wrote,
'Out on me lawn, an' stroke their pretty fur.
God bless yeh, boy.' An' then she ends 'er note,
'Yer dinkum cobber,' an' 'er moniker.
A sport? You bet! She's marri'd to an Earl—
An Aussie girl."

ACKNOWLEDGEMENTS

The selection of C. J. Dennis's verse in this book first appeared in the following works:

A Spring Song, The Intro, Doreen, Mar and *Beef Tea* appeared in THE SONGS OF A SENTIMENTAL BLOKE, first published in 1915 (A&R)

Ginger Mick (Introduction), War and *"A Gallant Gentleman"* appeared in THE MOODS OF GINGER MICK, first published in 1916 (A&R)

Joi, the Glug appeared in THE GLUGS OF GOSH, first published in 1917 (A&R)

Washing Day appeared in DOREEN, first published in 1917 (A&R)

A Digger's Tale appeared in DIGGER SMITH, first published in 1918 (A&R)

The Silent Member appeared in BACKBLOCK BALLADS AND LATER VERSES, first published in 1918 (A&R)

The Vision and *A Morning Song* appeared in JIM OF THE HILLS, first published in 1919 (A&R)

The Swagman, The Circus and *The Triantiwontigongolope* appeared in A BOOK FOR KIDS, first published in 1921 (A&R), later reissued as ROUNDABOUT

Green Walls appeared in THE SINGING GARDEN, first published in 1938 (A&R)

The Spoilers, To a Dead Mate (Henry Lawson) and *The Road's End* first appeared in RANDOM VERSE (Hallcraft, 1952)—a selection of C. J. Dennis verse from the *Herald,* Melbourne by his widow Margaret Herron.

A Post-Cup Tale and *Toolangi* first appeared in the *Herald,* Melbourne